BAKE, MAKE & LEARN TO COOK VEGETARIAN

Healthy & Green Recipes for Young Cooks

DAVID ATHERTON

illustrated by ALICE BOWSHER

CANDLEWICK PRESS

For my nieces and nephews: James, Louis, Mary-Joy, Charlotte, Joel, and Benjamin.
Eat your greens!
DA

For my Mum—thank you for always making a vegetarian option for me.
And for my Dad—thank you for trying my vegetarian cooking.
AB

Text copyright © 2021 by Nomadbaker Ltd.
Illustrations copyright © 2021 by Alice Bowsher
"The Great British Baking Show" Baker logo™ is licensed by Love Productions Ltd. All rights reserved.

No part of this book may be reproduced, transmitted, or stored in an information retrieval system in any form or by any means, graphic, electronic, or mechanical, including photocopying, taping, and recording, without prior written permission from the publisher.

First US edition 2022

Library of Congress Catalog Card Number 2021953450
ISBN 978-1-5362-2843-4

CCP 27 26 25 24 23 22
10 9 8 7 6 5 4 3 2 1

Printed in Shenzhen, Guangdong, China

This book was typeset in Alice, Hunterswood, and Vibur.
The illustrations were created digitally.

Candlewick Press
99 Dover Street
Somerville, Massachusetts 02144

www.candlewick.com

INTRODUCTION

My family is **vegetarian,** so I grew up eating food made with lots and lots of colorful vegetables. My mum—who's a fantastic cook—taught me that vegetarian food is easy to make and tastes delicious.

Thanks to my mum, I also learned that adding vegetables, fruits, and seeds to recipes can make them even more exciting. From cauliflower in your smoothie to pears in your muffins or even chia seeds in your crackers, this book is packed with recipes that have a tasty twist.

I've called the recipes in this book "green" because "eating green" means not only eating things that are green in color, but also eating healthy vegetables, fruits, and plants. AND we describe something as "green" if it is good for the planet too.

It's really important to learn about eating green, and you can share the fun by preparing the recipes with your friends and family. If you are already a star baker or a fancy cook, you can also add your personal touches to the recipes and create your own flavor combinations.

So, tie on your apron, and let's get going on another food adventure!

David

CONTENTS

Yummy Meals

Savory Snacks

Sweet Treats

Showstoppers

EATING GREEN

Homegrown food

Where does the food you eat come from? This is really important to think about when you're eating green. If food travels a long way by plane or by truck, it creates pollution, which is bad for our planet. Next time you buy fruits or vegetables, look where they've come from—there is usually a sign or sticker—and ask whether you can buy locally produced alternatives. Or how about trying to grow your own?

Seasonal food

Another way to eat green is to eat fruits and vegetables that are in season. This means eating foods when they ripen naturally. For example, in many places, apples are ready to pick in the late summer and early autumn and strawberries are ready starting in spring. Food out of season in your area has often traveled a long way, it might be full of pesticides or preservatives, and it might have been stored for a long time. Choosing seasonal food when you can means that you're more likely to eat cleaner, healthier foods.

Top tip: *Did you know that lots of farms allow you to pick your own fruits and vegetables? See if you can find one close to you and pick your own food to eat!*

Healthy foods

We need to eat lots of different kinds of food to make sure we're as healthy as we can be. Eating green doesn't just mean vegetables like broccoli, carrots, or potatoes, but also fruits, nuts, seeds, roots—and even edible flowers. I am vegetarian, and I still eat foods that come from animals, such as eggs, milk, or yogurt (I love yogurt). Some people are vegan, which means they don't eat any food that comes from an animal. Many of the recipes in this book are vegan, and for others, you can swap plant-based milk for cow's milk, soy spread for butter, vegan cheese for cheese made from dairy, and agave, rice, or date syrup for honey.

Before you get going

- It takes time to learn how to be safe in the kitchen. All the recipes in this book will need adult supervision—work together and have fun!

- If you have food allergies, or are cooking for someone with food allergies, you need to check the ingredients list carefully.

- Finally, I am a nurse, so it is especially important for me to remind you to wash and dry your hands before cooking.

PANTRY ESSENTIALS

A balanced diet includes carbohydrates, proteins, fats, and fiber as well as vitamins and minerals. I like to keep my pantry well-stocked with these ingredients to help me make nutritious and healthy recipes.

 Ground flaxseeds are shiny little seeds that are made into a powder. You can find them in your supermarket. They are sometimes called ground flaxseeds, ground linseeds, or flax meal, but they are all the same thing.

 Chia seeds are full of goodness. They get very sticky and soft when wet, which provides an important texture in baking.

 Nuts and seeds—take your pick! Sunflower seeds, almonds, and walnuts are all great for added protein, vitamins, and fiber in your food.

 Flours come in many different varieties. In this book, you'll find all-purpose, whole wheat, self-rising, buckwheat, and bread flours. If you don't have room in your pantry, just stick to a good all-purpose flour, a whole wheat flour, and a self-rising flour.

 Milk—the choice is yours. I usually use plant-based milks. The same goes for vegetable spreads or butters.

 Nut and seed butters are full of good fats that we need in our diet. I love peanut butter, but there are lots of different kinds, such as cashew, almond, or sunflower seed butter.

 Canned beans are a great source of vegetarian protein. They're full of fiber and B vitamins too.

 Grains like rice, wheat, and oats contain carbohydrates that give you more energy. If you can, try whole grains like brown rice, which are more nutritious.

 Herbs and spices are a pantry must! Try different flavors and find your favorites. I love turmeric, paprika, oregano, cumin, cinnamon . . . and more!

Weighing and measuring

- All recipes are measured in cups
- tsp = teaspoon
- tbsp = tablespoon
- oz = ounce
- The oven temperatures are in degrees Fahrenheit (°F).

A QUICK EQUIPMENT LIST

It's a good idea to check you have all the equipment needed for a recipe before you start. This is the equipment you will use in this book:

parchment paper

cookie sheet

mixing cup

cookie cutters

blender

cake pans

safety knife

cutting board

cooling rack

cupcake tin (12-hole)

electric mixer

food processor

frying pan (nonstick)

grater

large mixing bowl

measuring cup

measuring spoons

muffin tin (12-hole)

oven mitts

casserole dish

peeler

rolling pin

saucepan

sieve

spatula

spoon

immersion blender

scale

whisk

wok

YUMMY MEALS

MAGIC TOMATO SAUCE

This is my favorite sauce ever! It's so fresh and full of tasty vegetables. It can be used in all sorts of recipes—that's why it's magic! I make a fresh batch every week, then keep it in the fridge or freeze it. It's the perfect sauce for pasta, pizza, and so many meals.

Ingredients

Two 15 oz cans of
   diced tomatoes

¼ cup water

1 onion

1 medium carrot

2 sticks of celery

½ a green pepper

5 cloves of garlic

1 tsp salt

Makes 2 portions

Method

1 Pour both cans of tomatoes into a saucepan and add the water. Bring to a simmer over a medium heat.

2 Peel the onion and carrot and roughly chop, along with the celery and pepper, then add to the saucepan.

3 Finely grate the garlic and add this to the saucepan with the salt.

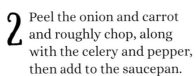

4 Simmer for 30 minutes over a medium heat.

5 Pour into a blender and whizz until smooth. Leave to cool.

6 Divide into 2 portions and keep in the fridge for up to 3 days, or freeze.

SPAGHETTI "BOLOGNESE"

This dish gets its name from a beautiful city in Italy called Bologna. Everyone has their own special recipe—and this is mine. Spaghetti is fun to eat because it is long, slippery, and slurpy, but there are lots of different pasta shapes and all of them go well with this delicious sauce.

Method

1 Add 1 portion of magic tomato sauce to a saucepan.

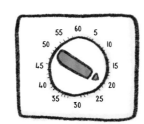

2 Add the lentils and oregano. Simmer over a low heat for 20 minutes, stirring frequently.

3 While your sauce is cooking, bring a large pot of water to boil, add the spaghetti, and simmer for 8–10 minutes. Then drain.

4 Serve the spaghetti with your "Bolognese" sauce and grated cheese.

Ingredients

1 portion of magic tomato sauce (p. 2)

¾ cup split red lentils (or cooked green lentils)

1 tsp dried oregano

½ box of spaghetti (8 oz)

2 oz cheddar cheese, grated

Makes 4 servings

EYE LOVE BREAD

Ingredients

3 cups bread flour,
    plus extra for
    dusting

1 tsp fast-acting yeast

1 tsp salt

1 small carrot

1 cup warm water

4 oz cheddar cheese

4 medium eggs

Makes 4 servings

This recipe is from one of my favorite countries—Georgia. It is a bread called *khachapuri* that is shaped like an eye with an egg in the middle. Have a look on the next page for some ideas to make your own version of this delicious "veggy" bread! Remember, dough needs a warm place and plenty of time to rise, so find a good book to read and relax for a bit. This tasty bread is worth the wait and makes a perfect lunch or dinner.

Serving suggestion

Serve your "veggy" bread with a delicious rainbow salad (p. 12) on the side.

Method

1 Put the flour, yeast, and salt into a large mixing bowl.

2 Finely grate the carrot and add to the flour. Pour in the warm water.

3 Mix with a spatula until it forms a sticky dough.

4 Cover with a tea towel and leave for 5 minutes.

5 Knead for 5 minutes. It might be very sticky, but don't worry (and don't add more flour).

6 Cover and leave in a warm place until it doubles in size (this may take more than an hour).

7 Preheat oven to 400°F.

8 Split the dough into 4 pieces. On a lightly floured surface, roll each one out to make a rectangle about 8 inches by 10 inches.

9 Roll the longer edge over once on each side and press the ends together to make an eye shape.

10 Repeat with the other pieces of dough, then transfer to a lined baking sheet. Coarsely grate the cheese on top.

11 Cover with tea towels and leave to rise for 20 minutes.

12 Bake for 8 minutes, then remove from the oven and crack an egg into each bread base.

13 Pop the bread back into the oven for 5 minutes until the egg is perfectly cooked.

Suggestions for fillings

Try adding your favorite veggies. Prepare your vegetables and oven-roast in a little oil for 20 minutes or until soft. Add to your bread base after step 11. You can try different fillings for each one—I like roasted peppers and mushrooms!

5

CHEESY NUTTY GNUDI

Gnudi (the *G* is silent like in the word *gnome*) are Italian dumplings that taste like fluffy, cheesy clouds. I like to serve mine with my homemade, nutty "pesto change-o" and a delicious green salad on the side.

Ingredients

2 medium eggs

¾ cup ricotta cheese

½ cup vegetarian Parmesan or pecorino cheese (grated)

½ cup all-purpose flour, plus extra for dusting

½ a jar of pesto change-o sauce (p. 24)

Makes 14 dumplings (2–4 servings)

Method

1 Whisk the eggs with a fork in a mixing bowl, then stir in the ricotta and Parmesan cheeses.

2 Add the flour until just combined (do not overmix).

3 Line a baking sheet with parchment paper and dust with lots of flour using a sieve.

4 Place teaspoonfuls of the mixture on the baking sheet.

5 Sprinkle more flour on top, then place in the fridge for 30 minutes.

6 Bring a large saucepan of water to boil.

7 Gently drop each gnudi into the boiling water, cooking about six at a time. Once they float to the top, they are cooked. Use a slotted spoon to scoop each batch onto a plate. Repeat until all the gnudi are cooked, then return them to the empty pot, stir in the pesto, and serve in bowls.

Serving suggestion

You can also serve the gnudi with magic tomato sauce (p. 2) and a sprinkle of cheese on top.

STIR-FRY NOODLES

I love stir-fry because it has oodles of soft noodles, crunchy vegetables, and a tasty, sticky sauce. You can choose whatever vegetables you like, but ones with a good crunch work best. My favorite part of this recipe is shaking up the sauce and dancing around the kitchen! A perfect speedy supper!

Ingredients

Sauce

1 clove of garlic (minced)

2 tbsp soy sauce

2 tbsp hoisin sauce

1 tbsp honey

1 tbsp nut butter

Stir-fry

1 red pepper

⅔ cup baby corn

2 tbsp vegetable oil
for frying

1 package of egg
noodles (12 oz)

½ cup frozen peas

1 cup snow peas

1 small bunch of fresh
cilantro or basil

Makes 4 servings

Method

1 Put all the sauce ingredients into a jar.

2 Screw on the lid and shake up and down until mixed!

3 Slice the red pepper into strips.

4 Slice the baby corn into quarters.

5 Add the oil to a wok or frying pan over a medium-high heat.

6 Add the pepper and baby corn to the wok and cook for 5 minutes, stirring every 30 seconds.

7 Cook the noodles according to the instructions on the package, and add the frozen peas to cook with them.

8 Add the snow peas to the wok and cook for another 2 minutes.

9 Drain the noodles and peas, then add to the wok and stir in. Add the sauce.

10 Pluck the cilantro or basil leaves from their stems and add. Keep stirring and fry for a final minute before serving.

Ingredients

1 cup spinach

1 ½ cups warm water

1 cup buckwheat flour

½ cup all-purpose flour

1 tsp fast-acting yeast

1 medium egg

1 tbsp olive oil
  for frying

Makes 8 crepes

Suggestions for fillings

Try spreading some pesto change-o (p. 24), creamy beany dip (p. 28), or pea-camole (p. 29) onto the crepes, then add grated cheese and chopped tomatoes or steamed broccoli.

GREEN SPINACH CREPES

When you mix all these ingredients together, you'll get a bowl of bubbling green batter, just like a witch's cauldron. This isn't a spooky potion though—it's a fantastic crepe mixture! My favorite way to eat these is with hummus and grated carrot, rolled up like a sausage, but you can try any filling you like.

Method

1 Put the spinach and water in a measuring cup and whizz with an immersion blender until it looks like green water.

2 In a mixing bowl, add the flours, yeast, egg, and the green water. Whisk until you have a smooth batter.

3 Cover and leave for 1 hour, until the batter looks bubbly.
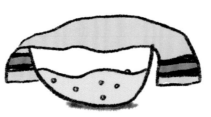

4 Brush a frying pan with a little oil. Heat over a medium-high heat and pour in a ladle of batter.

6 Transfer to a plate, fry the next crepe, and keep stacking.

5 Allow to cook for 2 minutes, then, using a spatula, flip the crepe and cook for 2 minutes on the other side.

7 Serve your crepes with different savory fillings!

RAINBOW SALAD

This crunchy salad is packed with colorful and tasty ingredients, and it's delicious tossed in a mango dressing. If you have any dressing left over, pour it into a jar and pop it in the fridge (it lasts for up to a week). I also like to dunk carrot and pepper slices into the dressing as a healthy go-to snack.

Ingredients

Rainbow salad

half a head of romaine lettuce

½ a red pepper

1 small carrot

2 oz cheddar cheese

1 cup canned kidney beans

½ cup canned corn
   (whole kernel)

Mango dressing

1 cup mango (peeled and
   diced)

1 tbsp white wine vinegar

1 tsp salt

1 tbsp honey

½ a clove of garlic (minced)

Makes 4 servings

Method

1 Wash the lettuce, pepper, and carrot in a colander.

2 Shake the lettuce dry, finely chop, and transfer to a bowl.

3 Dice the cheese and the red pepper into little cubes and add to the bowl.

4 Peel and grate the carrot and add to the salad.

5 Drain the beans and corn, and tip into the bowl.

6 To make the dressing, put all the ingredients in a mixing cup and blitz with an immersion blender until smooth.

7 Toss the salad together with the dressing and serve.

CORN & POTATO CAKES

My mum made these potato cakes when I was little, and I loved eating them with almost ALL my meals. What will you eat them with? Poached egg, mango chutney, and steamed broccoli? Veggie sausages and beans? Make the cakes into any shape you like. I do heart shapes because I ♥ them—and I think you will too!

Ingredients

1 medium carrot

1 lb russet potatoes

⅓ cup couscous

⅓ cup water (boiling)

1 ⅓ cup canned corn
  (whole kernel, drained)

1 tsp salt

1 tsp smoked paprika

1 medium egg

4 oz vegetarian Parmesan
  (or pecorino) cheese

A little flour for dusting

Makes 12 cakes

Method

1 Peel and dice the carrot and potatoes, then boil in a saucepan for 10–15 minutes.

2 Put the couscous into a bowl and add boiling water. Leave for 5 minutes.

3 Put half the corn into a food processor and blitz until roughly chopped up.

4 Drain the carrot and potatoes and roughly mash.

5 In a mixing bowl, add the blended corn, mashed carrots and potatoes, couscous, salt, smoked paprika, whole corn, and egg. Stir until combined.

6 Grate the cheese and add to the mixture.

7 Chill in the fridge for 20 minutes.

8 Preheat oven to 400°F.

9 Press out the potato mix on a lightly floured surface to ¾ inch thick.

10 Create shapes with your hands or a cookie cutter, and place the cakes on a lightly floured baking sheet.

11 Bake for 15–20 minutes, then leave to cool for 5 minutes before serving with your favorite meal.

VEGGIE BURGERS

Ingredients

1 cup canned black
    beans (drained)

1 medium (about
    4 oz) sweet potato
    (uncooked)

3 ½ oz firm tofu

2 oz cheddar cheese

2 tbsp bread flour, plus
    extra for dusting

½ tsp salt

1 tsp ground cumin

½ tsp garam masala

1 medium egg

1 tbsp olive oil for frying

Makes 10 burgers

These scrummy burgers are packed with protein and taste AMAZING with a slice of melted cheese on top. Impress your friends at a BBQ by serving these on a burger bun with the best sweet potato fries (p. 40) on the side. Or just eat them as a midweek treat—heaven on a plate!

Method

1 In a large mixing bowl, crush the black beans with your hands to break them up.

2 Peel and finely grate the uncooked sweet potato.

3 Mash the tofu with a fork.

4 Grate the cheddar cheese.

5 Add the cheese, tofu, and sweet potato to the beans, then add the flour, salt, cumin, garam masala, and egg.

6 Mix until well combined and then chill in the fridge for 30 minutes.

7 Divide the mixture into 10 equal portions. Roll each portion into a ball and press flat into a burger shape.

8 Put the burgers on a baking sheet lined with parchment paper, and dust with flour. Then chill in the fridge for 1 hour.

9 Add the olive oil to a frying pan over a medium heat and gently fry the burgers on each side for 10 minutes.

10 Serve on a burger bun with your favorite sauce and the best sweet potato fries on the side.

VEGGIE KORMA BOWL

Ingredients

1 medium sweet potato

2 peppers (any color)

1 small zucchini

1 portion of magic tomato
   sauce (p. 2)

1 can of coconut milk
   (13 ½ oz)

1 tsp turmeric

1 tsp salt

1 cup basmati rice

2 tsp garam masala

1 small bunch of fresh
   cilantro

Makes 4 servings

Some people like their curry hot and some people like it mild. Korma is traditionally a mild, creamy curry (just how I like it), but if you prefer it spicy, throw in some chili or add hot sauce at the end. Either way, it will taste simply delicious!

Method

1 Peel the sweet potato, then chop the peppers, zucchini, and sweet potato into ½-inch chunks.

2 Place the tomato sauce, coconut milk, turmeric, and salt in a medium saucepan and bring to a simmer.

3 Add the sweet potato, peppers, and zucchini to the curry sauce and gently simmer for 30 minutes until the vegetables are cooked through.

4 Meanwhile, place the rice into a small saucepan and cover with water, so it's ½ inch above the rice level. Set heat to medium.

5 As soon as you see the first bubbles of a simmer, put on a tight-fitting lid and turn down the heat to the lowest setting. Leave the rice to cook for 12 minutes (do not remove the lid).

6 Take the curry off the heat and stir through the garam masala.

7 Cut the cilantro with scissors (including the stalks).

8 Serve the rice in bowls, topped with the curry and sprinkled with cilantro. I like to serve mine with a big dollop of mango chutney too!

SPOOKY CARROT SOUP

This soup is the perfect treat for a chilly autumn day. It is sweet and smooth, with a spooky spiderweb topping. If you don't like spiders, the yogurt topping can look really pretty as a swirl. My speckled scones (p. 30) or bread crowns (p. 38) are perfect for dipping in the soup too!

Ingredients

1 lb carrots

2 tsp olive oil

½ tsp salt

1 portion of magic
 tomato sauce (p. 2)

4 cups water

⅓ cup plain yogurt

A squeeze of lemon
 (to taste)

A small packet of
 pumpkin seeds

Makes 4 servings

Method

1 Preheat oven to 400°F.

2 Peel the carrots and cut into ½-inch rounds.

3 Place the carrots on a baking sheet with the oil and salt, and toss until coated.

4 Roast the carrots for 30 minutes until soft.

5 Pour the tomato sauce and water into a medium saucepan and bring to a gentle simmer.

6 Put the roasted carrots and tomato sauce into a blender. Make sure the lid is on tight so the hot mixture won't splatter, and whizz until smooth.

7 Spoon the yogurt into a piping or sandwich bag, then add a squeeze of lemon and mix it in.

8 Pour the soup into bowls, then snip off a corner of the piping or sandwich bag and create a swirl on top of the soup.

9 Take a toothpick and drag lines from the center of the swirl out to the edges to create the web.

10 Add pumpkin-seed "flies" to your web. Serve with a witch's cackle and a speckled scone or bread crown.

Ingredients

1 large sweet potato
   (about 8 oz)

½ lb cauliflower (about half a
   head)

½ lb broccoli

½ box of macaroni
   or small-shell pasta (8 oz)

1 ½ tbsp butter

¼ cup all-purpose flour

2 cups milk

1 cup cheddar cheese (grated)

½ tsp salt

½ tsp garam masala

½ tsp smoked paprika
   (optional)

Makes 6 servings

CHEESY VEGGIE BAKE

This creamy, cheesy, veggie-packed bake is the perfect comfort food. It makes you happy and warm when you eat it. I like to use broccoli, cauliflower, and sweet potato in this dish, but you can choose your favorite vegetables. If you don't use all the cauliflower, why not try my cauli hot wings recipe on page 34?

Method

1 Peel and chop the sweet potato into ¾-inch chunks and cut the cauliflower and broccoli into small florets.

2 Bring water to a boil in a large saucepan. Add pasta and veggies, reduce heat, and simmer for 10 minutes.

3 Drain everything and place the veggies and pasta in a casserole dish.

4 Preheat oven to 400°F.

5 Melt the butter in a saucepan over a low heat. Add the flour, stirring with a whisk for 1 minute until combined.

6 Add ½ cup of the milk, and whisk to bring the mixture together (don't worry if it goes lumpy).

7 Turn up to a medium heat. As the sauce thickens, add more milk and keep whisking until you have used all the milk and the lumps are gone.

8 Add ¾ cup of the grated cheese to the sauce along with the salt and garam masala. Combine together with the whisk.

9 Pour the sauce over the pasta and vegetables, and sprinkle the rest of the cheese (and smoked paprika, if you are using) on top.

10 Bake for 15–20 minutes until it is golden and bubbling on top.

11 Once out of the oven, allow to cool for 5 minutes before serving.

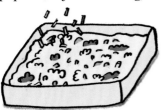

PESTO CHANGE-O!

Pesto is a brilliant way of adding flavor to almost any meal or snack. I like spreading it on sandwiches, tossing it with pasta, dolloping it on cheese scones, splattering it over pancakes—and more! Try different nuts and herbs to find your favorite pesto mix.

Ingredients

1 clove of garlic (minced)

⅓ cup nuts (your choice, but I love walnuts, pistachios, or cashews)

1 oz vegetarian Parmesan (or pecorino) cheese

¼ cup olive oil

1 bunch of fresh basil

¼ cup spinach

Makes 1 small jar

Method

1 Put the garlic, nuts, and cheese into a food processor and whizz until the nuts are really broken up.

2 Add the olive oil and whizz again until it forms a paste.

3 Add the basil (stalks as well) and the spinach, then pulse until smooth (but so that you can still see bits of leaves). Pour into a jar and keep in the fridge for up to 3 days.

Serving suggestions

Serve with gnudi (p. 6), on your crepes (p. 10), in your birds' nests (p. 35), or even as a sandwich spread (p. 38).

gnudi

crepes

birds' nests

sandwich spread

SAVORY SNACKS

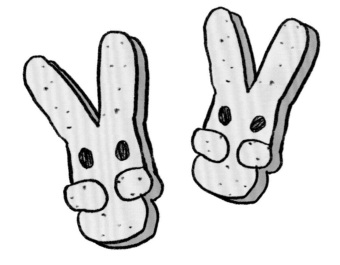

CHEESY RABBIT CRACKERS

Ingredients

4 tbsp (half stick) butter

1 cup all-purpose flour,
   plus extra for dusting

2 tbsp whole wheat flour

3 oz cheddar cheese

2 tbsp chia seeds

20 raisins, for decoration

Makes 20 crackers

These crackers are deliciously cheesy with a golden crunch. A perfect snack for afternoon munching! I love making these rabbit shapes with big ears to scoop up my two favorite dips (pp. 28–29). You can try lots of different shapes too. What will you make?

Method

1 Cut the butter into cubes, then rub into the flours until it resembles breadcrumbs.

2 Grate in the cheese.

3 Add the chia seeds.

4 Mix everything together until it forms a dough. You might need to sprinkle in a little water if the mixture is very dry, but be careful not to add too much.

5 Wrap and chill in the fridge for 30 minutes.

6 Preheat oven to 350°F.

7 On a lightly floured surface, roll out the dough to at least ¼ inch thick (or thicker, if you prefer).

8 Cut out the crackers with a small person-shaped cookie cutter (4 inches). Fold in the arms and transfer to a lined baking sheet. The legs are now your bunny ears!

9 Cut the raisins in half and put 2 halves on each cracker for the eyes, just below the ears.

10 Bake for 12–15 minutes, then allow to cool. Serve with some yummy dips!

CREAMY BEANY DIP

This dip can be made with lots of different beans. Have fun and experiment! Kidney beans will give you a pink dip, and black beans will make it black. The important thing to remember is to whizz, whizz, whizz until the dip is smooth and creamy. Serve with carrot sticks, cheesy rabbit crackers (p. 26), or bread crowns (p. 38)!

Ingredients

½ a clove of garlic

1 can cannellini beans
    (15 oz, drained)

½ cup cottage cheese

½ tsp smoked paprika

2 tbsp light tahini or
    olive oil

1 tsp salt

Makes 1 bowl

Method

1 Crush the garlic and transfer to a food processor.

2 Add the rest of the ingredients to the food processor and whizz until smooth.

3 Serve with your choice of crunchy vegetables or crackers and enjoy!

PEA-CAMOLE

Guacamole is a Mexican dish known for its very strong flavors. This version includes petits pois—small, sweet peas that make it smooth and sweet. It's perfect for dipping with cheesy crackers, and it makes a great sandwich spread too!

Ingredients

1 cup frozen petits pois (petite peas)

1 large avocado

½ tsp salt

1 tbsp olive oil

½ lime (juiced)

A small bunch of fresh cilantro

Makes 1 bowl

Method

1 Put the frozen petits pois into a bowl and cover with boiling water. Leave for 3 minutes.

2 Drain the peas, and tip into a blender.

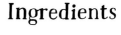

3 Carefully cut the avocado in half, remove the stone, then peel.

4 Add half the avocado to the blender, along with the salt, oil, and lime juice. Whizz until smooth and then scrape into a mixing bowl.

5 Mash the other avocado half on a plate with a fork.

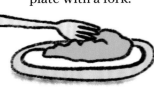

6 Add the mashed avocado to the bowl and mix it all together. Chop the cilantro leaves and sprinkle on top.

Ingredients

3 ½ cups self-rising flour, plus
    extra for dusting

1 tsp baking powder

½ tsp salt

2 tbsp poppy seeds

6 tbsp unsalted butter

1 ripe plantain

2 ½ oz cheddar cheese

¾ cup milk (plus a little
    extra to brush the scones)

Makes 25 scones

SPECKLED SCONES

These cheesy scones are beautifully soft and speckled with poppy seeds. I make mine with plantain, a type of banana popular in Africa and the Caribbean. Once the scones have cooled, split them in half and spread a little butter on them, or dunk them into some spooky carrot soup (p. 20).

Method

1 Preheat oven to 400°F.

2 Put the flour, baking powder, salt, and poppy seeds into a bowl.

3 Cut the butter into cubes, then rub into the flour mix until it resembles breadcrumbs.

4 Coarsely grate the plantain and cheese, then stir into the flour mixture.

5 Stir in the milk and bring it together to form a ball of dough (don't worry if it is a little sticky).

6 On a lightly floured surface, roll out the dough until it is ¾ inch thick.

7 Cut out the scones with a 2-inch cookie cutter and place on a lined baking sheet.

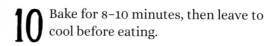

8 Continue until you've used up all the dough (about 25 scones).

10 Bake for 8–10 minutes, then leave to cool before eating.

9 Brush the tops of the scones with the extra milk.

MOON POCKETS

These yummy savory pocket pies are made with sweet potato, but you can try lots of different fillings. What about roasted peppers and chickpeas? Or carrots and potatoes? You can experiment with more or less garam masala and try other spices like curry powder for something a little hotter.

Ingredients

4 tbsp unsalted butter

1 cup all-purpose flour, plus extra for dusting

2 tbsp whole wheat flour

1 medium sweet potato

1 medium egg

1 can of corn (8 ¾ oz, drained)

1 tsp garam masala

½ tsp salt

1 tbsp olive oil for frying

2 tbsp poppy seeds

Makes 14 pies

Method

1 Cut the butter into cubes and then, with your fingers, rub into the two flours until it resembles breadcrumbs.

2 Peel and finely grate the sweet potato, and add half to the flour mix.

3 Crack the egg over a clean bowl and tip the yolk from shell to shell, letting the egg white run into the bowl (save this for later). Add the yolk to the flour mixture.

4 Bring the flour mixture into a dough (add a little water if necessary, but not too much).

5 Wrap and chill in the fridge for 30 minutes.

6 Add the rest of the sweet potato, corn, garam masala, and salt to a frying pan with a little oil over a low heat. Cook for 10 minutes, stirring every minute.

7 Preheat oven to 350°F.

8 Roll out the dough to at least ¼ inch thick (a bit thinner if you can), then cut out circles with a 4-inch cookie cutter.

9 Put a teaspoon of sweet potato mix from the frying pan in the middle of each circle.

10 Fold each circle over and press gently to seal. Crimp the edges with a fork.

11 Place on a lined baking sheet, brush with the egg white, and sprinkle with poppy seeds.

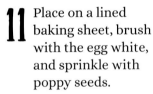

12 Bake for 15 minutes, leave to cool, then serve!

Ingredients

Small head of cauliflower

2 tbsp all-purpose flour

2 tbsp milk

2 tbsp water

½ tsp smoked paprika

¼ tsp salt

½ cup breadcrumbs

Makes 4 servings

CAULI HOT WINGS

These cauliflower bites have the perfect crunch and are just as delicious as chicken hot wings. Add them as a tasty side dish to a meal, or munch them as a snack with some pea-camole (p. 29).

Method

1 Preheat oven to 350°F.

2 Cut the cauliflower into little florets.

3 To make the batter, put the flour, milk, water, smoked paprika, and salt into a bowl and mix until smooth.

4 Tip the breadcrumbs onto a plate.

5 Dip the florets into the batter, then roll in the breadcrumbs.

6 Place the florets on a lined baking sheet (make sure they're not touching) and bake for 20 minutes.

7 Give your florets a little shake and turn them over with tongs.

8 Bake again for 15 minutes.

9 Serve your cauli hot wings with your favorite dip!

BIRDS' NESTS

Tweet, tweet! You'll have loads of fun making these super-easy birds' nests. The filo pastry makes the base really crispy and crunchy, and the mini mozzarella balls look like tiny eggs, just like in a real nest.

Ingredients

1 tsp vegetable oil to grease the pan

4 sheets of filo pastry

8 tbsp of pesto change-o (p. 24)

8 cherry tomatoes

16 mini mozzarella balls

Makes 8 nests

Method

1 Preheat oven to 300°F.

2 Brush 8 holes of a 12-hole muffin tin with vegetable oil.

3 Stack the 4 filo pastry sheets and roll into a sausage shape.

4 Carefully, with a sharp knife, cut slices that are ¼ inch thick.

5 Tease out the filo strands so they look like spaghetti. Divide into 8 portions.

6 Tangle the filo strands together to make 8 nests. Make a big hollow in the middle of the nests, and put them in the muffin tin.

7 Bake for 8 minutes.

8 Drizzle the inside of each nest with a tablespoon of pesto, then add a tomato and 2 mini mozzarella balls. You're ready to serve your nests!

MINI PIZZA SWIRLS

Ingredients

2 ½ cups bread flour, plus
   extra for dusting

½ cup whole wheat flour

1 tsp instant yeast

1 tsp salt

¾ cup warm water

1 tbsp olive oil to grease the pan

¼ cup tomato puree

2 tbsp water

1 tsp dried oregano

3 oz mozzarella cheese

Makes 10–12 pizzas

These mini pizza swirls are much easier to carry around than a big flat, floppy pizza, so they're perfect for a lunch box or a snack to take on the go. Have a look on the next page for suggestions for extra fillings. YUM!

Method

1 In a mixing bowl, combine the flours, yeast, salt, and ¾ cup warm water until it forms a dough. Cover with a tea towel and allow to sit for 10 minutes.

2 Knead the dough on a lightly floured surface for 5 minutes (do not add lots of flour—it doesn't matter if it starts off sticky).

3 Place the dough in a clean bowl and cover with a tea towel. Leave in a warm place until it doubles in size (about 25 minutes).

6 Mix the tomato puree, 2 tbsp of water, and oregano until combined, then spread onto the dough.

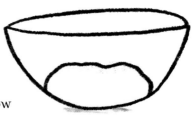

4 Lightly grease a 12-hole muffin tin.

5 Press the air out of the dough. Roll it out to make a rectangle about 8 inches by 12 inches.

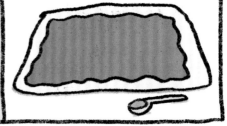

Suggestions for fillings

Once you get to step 7, sprinkle on your favorite veggies. Why not try thin slices of mushrooms or even grated carrot?

7 Grate the cheese and sprinkle on top. You can add any extra veggies now!

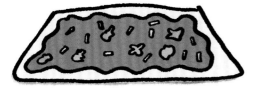

8 Roll the dough up into a long sausage and then cut into 10 pieces.

9 Arrange each piece in one of the holes of the muffin tin, cover with a tea towel, and leave in a warm place until they double in size (about 25 minutes).

10 Preheat oven to 400°F.

11 Sprinkle with a little extra cheese and bake for 12 minutes. Allow to cool a little before serving.

BREAD CROWNS

Ingredients

2 ½ cups bread flour,
   plus extra for dusting
½ cup whole wheat
   flour
1 tsp fast-acting yeast
½ tsp ground turmeric
1 tsp salt
¾ cup warm water

Makes 8 crowns

If I was going to crown the queen of all food, it would be bread. I eat bread every day (usually with peanut butter). So I wanted to make bread fit for royalty. Turmeric is a spice that is good for you, and when added to bread dough it turns really yellow, which is perfect for a crown.

Method

1 Mix the flours, yeast, turmeric, salt, and water together until it forms a dough.

2 Cover with a tea towel and allow to sit for 10 minutes.

3 Knead the dough on a lightly floured surface for 5 minutes (it doesn't matter if it starts off sticky—don't add too much flour).

4 Cover with a tea towel and leave in a warm place until it doubles in size (about 1 hour).

5 Divide the dough into 8 pieces and roll into balls.

6 Stick 2 fingers through the middle of each ball, then stretch your fingers apart to open up the hole.

7 Spin the circle of dough on your fingers to open up the hole to about 1 ½ inches wide.

8 Put them on a lined baking sheet, cover, and leave to rise until they double in size (about 30 minutes).

9 Preheat oven to 400°F.

10 Use scissors to snip all around the ring.

11 Bake for 12 minutes and leave to cool.

12 Serve with spooky carrot soup (p. 20), or pesto change-o (p. 24) and cheese, or your yummy dips (pp. 28–29).

THE BEST SWEET POTATO FRIES

Ingredients

2 medium sweet potatoes

1 tbsp cornstarch

½ tsp salt

2 tbsp vegetable oil

½ tsp smoked paprika
(optional)

Makes 4 servings

Who wants normal fries when you can have the best sweet potato fries?! These are perfect as a snack or as part of a main meal. Be careful: if you cook these too close together, they go soft, and we want them crispy!

Method

1 Preheat oven to 425°F.

2 Peel the sweet potatoes and cut into 2-inch strips.

3 Toss in a large mixing bowl with the cornstarch, salt, and oil.

4 Spread the fries onto a lined baking sheet and make sure they don't touch each other. Use two sheets if necessary.

5 Cook for 20 minutes and then check the fries.

6 Shake the fries. If any are brown at the edges, move them to the middle of the sheet.

7 Bake for another 10 minutes.

8 Once out of the oven, sprinkle with the smoked paprika. These fries are perfect on their own, with dips (pp. 28–29), or as a side to veggie burgers (p. 16).

SWEET TREATS

SUPER STRAWBERRY JAM

My super strawberry jam is used in so many recipes in this book: in my jam tarts (p. 43), on top of rice pudding (p. 52), and on my pink scones (p. 56) and spring butterfly cupcakes (p. 60). But my favorite way to enjoy it is spread on toast! This jam uses the magic of chia seeds, which go soft and sticky when wet.

Ingredients

16 oz strawberries,
   fresh or frozen

4 tsp sugar (optional)

2 tbsp chia seeds

1 tsp lemon juice

Makes 1 jar

Method

1 Remove stems and place strawberries in saucepan. Taste one strawberry to see how sweet they are.

2 Gently stir the strawberries over a low heat for 5 minutes. Take off the heat and crush with a potato masher.

3 Simmer for another 5 minutes. (If the strawberry didn't taste very sweet in step 1, add the sugar now.)

4 Take off the heat. Stir in the chia seeds and lemon juice.

5 Allow to cool, then transfer to a jar with a lid.

6 Keep in the fridge and use within a week.

JAM TARTS

Here's a recipe for jam tarts, using—you guessed it—my super strawberry jam! Or you can try adding yogurt and fruit, chocolate spread, and even peanut butter for the filling.

Ingredients

½ cup powdered sugar

¾ cup all-purpose flour, plus extra for dusting

½ cup whole wheat flour

6 tbsp unsalted butter

1 medium egg

Super strawberry jam (p. 42)

Makes 12 tarts

Method

1 Sift the powdered sugar into a mixing bowl and add the flours. Cut the butter into cubes and then, with your fingers, rub into the flour mixture until it resembles breadcrumbs.

2 Crack the egg over a clean bowl and tip the yolk from shell to shell, letting the egg white run into the bowl. Add the yolk to the flour mix and combine until it forms a ball of dough.

 **3** Wrap and leave in the fridge for 30 minutes.

4 Preheat oven to 400°F.

5 On a lightly floured surface, roll out the dough to ¼ inch thick. Cut out 12 discs with a 4-inch round cookie cutter.

6 Place each disc in a hole in a 12-hole cupcake pan, then prick the base with a fork a few times.

7 Chill in the fridge for 15 minutes.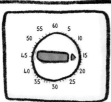

8 Bake for 15–20 minutes (until golden), then allow to cool before removing from the tin.

9 Spoon a teaspoonful of super strawberry jam into each pastry case.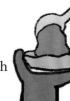

APPLE ROCK CAKES

I used to love picking apples when I was little, and these rock cakes were one of my favorite treats to bake. They stay fresh for a couple of days—in an airtight container—and are easy to take on an apple-picking picnic adventure!

Ingredients

2 medium apples

1 ½ cups self-rising flour

⅓ cup whole wheat flour

1 tsp baking powder

1 tsp ground cinnamon

¼ cup granulated sugar, plus extra for sprinkling

8 tbsp (1 stick) unsalted butter

2 tbsp raisins

1 medium egg

1 ½ tbsp milk

1 tsp vanilla extract

Makes 12 cakes

Method

1 Peel the apples, chop into ½-inch pieces, and put in a bowl of cold water.

2 Preheat oven to 350°F.

3 Put the flours, baking powder, cinnamon, and sugar into a mixing bowl. Cut the butter into cubes and rub into the mixture until it resembles breadcrumbs.

4 Drain the apples. Add them, along with the raisins, to the flour mixture and stir.

5 In a separate small bowl, mix the egg, milk, and vanilla extract together with a fork.

6 Add the egg mixture to the dry mixture and bring together to form a dough.

7 Take big tablespoonfuls of the mixture, then place on a lined baking sheet and sprinkle with sugar.

8 Bake for 12–15 minutes, then allow to cool on a cooling rack.

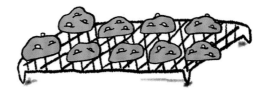

CHOCOLATE COOKIES

Some cookies are crunchy, some are chewy, and some melt in your mouth—just like these. Decorate them with chocolate chips and chewy raisins to make a treat full of avo-choco-goodness.

Ingredients

1 ripe avocado
   (about 4 oz)

½ cup brown sugar

2 ½ tbsp ground flax meal

1 tsp vanilla extract

¼ cup cocoa powder

½ cup all-purpose flour

½ tsp baking soda

3 tbsp raisins

¼ cup milk chocolate
   chips

Makes 10 cookies

Method

1 Preheat oven to 350°F.

2 Carefully cut the avocado in half, remove the stone, then peel. Add to a mixing bowl and whizz with an immersion blender. Add the sugar, flax meal, and vanilla extract, and whizz again.

3 Add the cocoa powder, flour, and baking soda, and whizz until smooth.

4 Using a tablespoon, place dollops of the mixture onto a lined baking sheet. Press the back of the spoon on top of each dollop to make a circle.

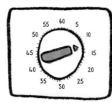

7 Cool on a cooling rack before eating—yum!

5 Decorate with the raisins and chocolate chips.

6 Bake for 12–15 minutes.

FREEZY GRAPES

These freezy treats taste just like sorbet. When you cover the grapes in yogurt and crunchy sprinkles, you get sour, sweet, and juicy all in one bite! They're a refreshing summer snack, but I like to eat them all year round.

Method

1 Line a baking sheet with parchment paper.

2 Put a grape onto a toothpick and dip into the yogurt.

3 Sprinkle your freeze-dried strawberry pieces (or edible decorations) over the yogurt-covered grape, rotating the toothpick as you go.

4 Gently place the grape on the sheet and release it with another toothpick. Repeat with all the grapes. Place the sheet in the freezer.

5 Freeze overnight, then transfer to a freezer bag. Keep in the freezer and eat as an icy treat!

Ingredients

40 red grapes

½ cup of strawberry yogurt

Freeze-dried strawberry pieces (or other edible sprinkles)

Makes 40 freezy grapes

LEMON & PEAR MUFFINS

These fruity, zesty muffins are so soft and fluffy, it's hard to eat just one! I make mine with pears and lemon, but you could try swapping the lemon for a lime.

Ingredients

1 lemon

1 can of pear halves in juice (15 oz)

⅓ cup rolled oats

⅓ cup granulated sugar

1 tbsp honey

3 tbsp light olive oil

2 medium eggs

1 ⅔ cups all-purpose flour

½ cup whole wheat flour

2 tsp baking powder

1 tbsp poppy seeds

Extra granulated or turbinado sugar for sprinkling on top

Makes 12 muffins

Method

1 Zest the lemon and set the zest aside. Place an empty bowl on a kitchen scale and press zero.

2 Juice the lemon into the bowl. Add the juice from the can of pears until the mixture weighs 3 ½ oz.

3 Add the lemon and pear juice to a small saucepan, along with the oats, and simmer gently for 3 minutes on the lowest heat until the oats are soft.

4 Preheat oven to 400°F.

5 Put the oat mixture into a food processor with the pear halves, sugar, honey, and oil, and blend until smooth.

6 Add the eggs and blend again until smooth.

7 In a mixing bowl, combine the flours, baking powder, poppy seeds, and lemon zest.

8 Pour the blended pear mixture into the flour mixture and stir until combined.

9 Prepare a 12-hole muffin tin with cupcake liners. Spoon the mixture into the liners until they're three-quarters full, then sprinkle with the extra sugar.

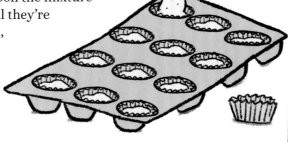

10 Bake for 5 minutes at 400°F. After 5 minutes, drop the temperature to 350°F and bake for a further 15 minutes. Leave to cool on a cooling rack, then serve.

STICKY FLAPJACK

Ingredients

8 tbsp butter (1 stick)

¼ cup light corn syrup

¾ cup dates

⅓ cup dried apricots (chopped)

⅓ cup raisins

⅓ cup sliced almonds

3 tbsp sunflower seeds

1 ⅔ cups rolled oats

¼ cup whole wheat flour

Makes 16 flapjacks

Who is Jack, and why is she flappy? I have no idea why these yummy oat bars are called flapjacks here in England, but they're one of my faves. This version is super-sticky and chewy—just how I like it. For a special breakfast, I crumble the flapjack into a bowl of plain yogurt with some chopped fruit. Delicious!

Method

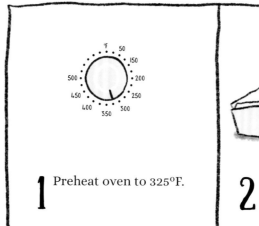

1 Preheat oven to 325°F.

2 Line an 8-inch square pan with parchment paper.

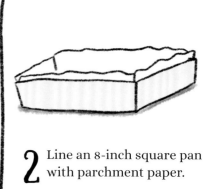

3 Melt the butter and corn syrup in a small saucepan over a low heat.

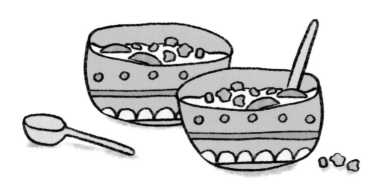

 **4** Put the dates into a food processor, add the melted butter and syrup, and blitz until smooth.

  **5** Add the apricots, raisins, almonds, sunflower seeds, oats, and flour into a mixing bowl.

 **6** Pour in the sticky date mixture and stir with a spatula until everything is coated.

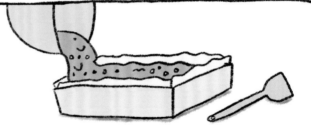 **7** Pour into the pan and push down with a spatula until level.

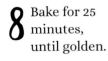 **8** Bake for 25 minutes, until golden.

 **9** Allow to cool before removing from the tin and cutting into squares.

RICE PUDDING

I loved it when my grandma used to make me this delicious, comforting dish. She baked hers in the oven, but my version is stirred on the stove. Rice pudding is great on its own, but I like to add honey and top it with a big dollop of my super strawberry jam (p. 42). Look on the next page for some other ideas to tickle your taste buds.

Ingredients

⅓ cup pudding rice
   (or risotto rice)
2 ½ cups milk
½ cup water
2 tbsp honey
Super strawberry jam,
   to serve (p. 42)

Makes 2 servings

Method

1 Add the rice, milk, water, and honey to a medium saucepan and bring to a gentle simmer (small bubbles) while stirring.

2 Put a lid on the pan and simmer for 40 minutes, giving it a stir every 5 minutes. You might want to use a timer so you don't forget. Be careful it doesn't boil over!

3 If it gets too thick before 40 minutes is up, add some more milk. It should be gloopy, not solid.

4 Top with a big dollop of super strawberry jam and serve!

Try these tasty variations

Chocolatey rice pudding

Add 2 teaspoons of cocoa powder and 1 teaspoon of vanilla extract to the saucepan before simmering. Once served, drop a few squares of chocolate on top and wait for them to melt.

Tropical rice pudding

Add ¼ cup of dried mango and 1 tablespoon of shredded coconut to the saucepan before simmering, and top with a fresh mango, peeled and chopped into chunks.

Spicy rice pudding

Add 1 tablespoon of raisins and 1 teaspoon of ground cinnamon to the saucepan before simmering. When served, grate an apple on top and sprinkle with some turbinado sugar.

ICE-DREAM SMOOTHIE

I dream of ice cream! You will be amazed that this is made from whizzed-up cauliflower. It's so creamy and the mango makes it super-sweet. You can try swapping the mango for other fruits like banana or pineapple.

Ingredients

1 mango
(about 7 oz)
4 cauliflower florets
(about 4 oz)
4 tbsp plain yogurt
2 tsp honey
Fresh fruit, to serve

Makes 4 servings

Method

1 Cut the mango in half lengthwise and carefully remove the stone. Remove the peel and chop the mango into ¾-inch chunks. Place on a baking sheet.

2 Add the cauliflower florets (don't use the stalky bits). Freeze for at least 3 hours (best frozen overnight).

3 Using a food processor, blend the frozen mango, cauliflower, yogurt, and honey until smooth.

4 Transfer to bowls and top with fresh fruit. Yum!

POPPED CHOCS

Ingredients

1 tbsp vegetable oil

3 tbsp popcorn kernels

7 oz dark or milk chocolate

¼ cup peanut butter

½ cup raisins (or other dried fruit)

¼ cup unsalted peanuts

Makes 20 chocs

Take some popcorn kernels (this is the name for a grain of corn), heat them in hot oil, and—pipperty, popperty, pop—you have a pan full of soft, puffed popcorn. The only thing to make it more delicious is to cover it in chocolate, of course!

Method

1 Put the oil and 3 kernels in a saucepan over a medium heat. When they pop, put the rest of the kernels in and quickly put on a tight-fitting lid.

2 Wait until you can't hear any more popping, then transfer to a mixing bowl.

3 Break up the chocolate and put into a heatproof bowl with the peanut butter.

4 Sit the bowl over a pan of barely simmering water and allow the chocolate to melt, stirring occasionally.

5 Pour the chocolate mixture onto the popcorn, and add the raisins and nuts. Give it a good stir.

6 Place tablespoonfuls of the mixture onto a lined baking sheet, then pop in the fridge to cool and set before eating.

Ingredients

2 cooked beets
(about 4 oz)

⅓ cup milk

3 cups self-rising flour,
plus extra for dusting

1 tsp baking powder

¼ cup granulated sugar

1 tsp vanilla extract

6 tbsp butter

To serve

Super strawberry jam (p. 42)

1 cup plain Greek yogurt

9 medium strawberries

Powdered sugar, to dust

Makes 12 scones

STRAWBERRY PINK SCONES

Everything looks better in pink! And these scones are no exception. They are perfect for an afternoon tea party and, served with your homemade super strawberry jam (p. 42), are sure to impress your friends!

Method

1 Finely grate the beets into a bowl and add the milk.

2 Add the flour, baking powder, sugar, and vanilla extract to a large mixing bowl. Cut the butter into cubes and then, with your fingers, rub into the mix until it resembles breadcrumbs.

3 Pour in the milk-and-beet mixture.

4 Mix until it forms a dough and let it sit for 10 minutes.

5 Preheat oven to 350°F.

6 On a floured surface, roll out the dough until it is ¾ inch thick.

7 Cut out the scones using a large cookie cutter.

8 Transfer to a lined baking sheet and bake for 12–15 minutes.

9 Leave to cool on a cooling rack.

10 Slice the scones in half, spread with jam, and put a dollop of yogurt in the middle.

11 Cut the strawberries into quarters and decorate each scone with three pieces.

12 Dust with the powdered sugar to finish.

Ingredients

2 oz white chocolate

1 cup dried apricots

⅓ cup walnuts

⅓ cup shredded coconut,
  plus extra for decoration

¼ cup rolled oats

Makes 20 snowballs

NUTTY SNOWBALLS

These balls are small but give you a mighty burst of energy! If you're going to a dance class, cycling in the park, or if you want to beat your friends in a snowball fight, then this is the snack for you!

Method

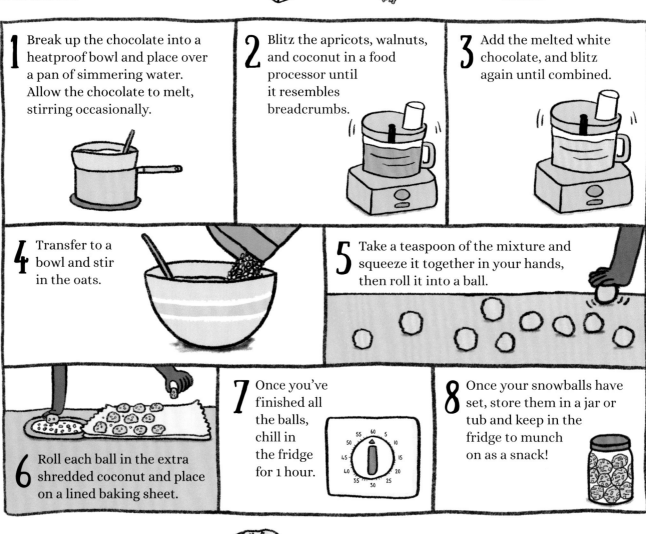

1 Break up the chocolate into a heatproof bowl and place over a pan of simmering water. Allow the chocolate to melt, stirring occasionally.

2 Blitz the apricots, walnuts, and coconut in a food processor until it resembles breadcrumbs.

3 Add the melted white chocolate, and blitz again until combined.

4 Transfer to a bowl and stir in the oats.

5 Take a teaspoon of the mixture and squeeze it together in your hands, then roll it into a ball.

6 Roll each ball in the extra shredded coconut and place on a lined baking sheet.

7 Once you've finished all the balls, chill in the fridge for 1 hour.

8 Once your snowballs have set, store them in a jar or tub and keep in the fridge to munch on as a snack!

SHOWSTOPPERS

SPRING BUTTERFLY CUPCAKES

It takes a little bit of practice to make the wings on these pretty cupcakes look just like butterflies. I practiced a lot and won first prize in a local baking competition when I was eight (which I'm still very proud of).

Ingredients

Cakes

1 cup frozen petite peas

8 tbsp (1 stick) unsalted butter (diced)

3 tbsp Greek yogurt

2 medium eggs

½ cup granulated sugar

3 tsp vanilla extract

1 ½ cups self-rising flour

1 tsp baking powder

Topping

9 tbsp unsalted butter (at room temperature)

1 tsp vanilla extract

2 ¼ cups powdered sugar, plus extra for dusting

2 tbsp Greek yogurt

12 tsp super strawberry jam (p. 42)

Colorful edible sprinkles

Makes 12 cakes

Method

1 Simmer the frozen peas in boiling water for 5 minutes.

2 Drain the peas and leave them in a bowl of cold water for 5 minutes.

3 Preheat oven to 350°F.

4 Prepare a 12-hole cupcake pan with cupcake liners.

5 Drain the peas and whizz in a blender with the butter, yogurt, eggs, sugar, and vanilla extract until smooth.

6 Sift the flour and baking powder into a bowl and add the mixture from the blender. Stir carefully until combined.

7 Divide the mixture between the cupcake liners (no more than two-thirds full).

8 Bake for 15 minutes, then cool on a cooling rack.

9 For the icing, whisk the butter with the vanilla extract and powdered sugar until smooth. Then mix in the Greek yogurt.

10 Once cool, cut out a circle from the top of each cake, leaving a small hole, and set aside.

11 Put a teaspoon of jam in each hole, followed by a generous dollop of the icing.

12 Cut the cake tops in half and stick them into the icing like butterfly wings. Dust with powdered sugar and decorate with sprinkles.

SUMMER SANDCASTLE CAKE

Ingredients

Cake

1 cup granulated sugar

1 cup brown sugar

1 ¼ cup vegetable oil

6 medium eggs

12 oz peeled carrots
  (or parsnips)

2 ¾ cups all-purpose flour

4 tsp baking powder

2 tsp cinnamon

Icing

8 tbsp unsalted butter
  (1 stick, room temperature)

2 cups powdered sugar

2 tsp vanilla extract

4 oz cream cheese
  (room temperature)

Toppings and decorations

12 graham cracker squares

About 12 toothpicks

4 oz marzipan

A small sheet of rice paper

Makes 14–16 servings

I grew up in a seaside town and loved going down to the beach to make sandcastles. The sand on this castle is made from whizzed-up graham crackers and inside is a delicious carrot cake. Just like a sandcastle, you can choose to decorate as you like! This is a BIG cake, so make sure you have a large mixing bowl.

Method

1 Preheat oven to 325°F.

2 Grease and dust two 8-inch round pans with a little flour. It helps to line the bottoms with parchment paper too.

3 In a large mixing bowl, beat the sugars, oil, and eggs until smooth.

4 Finely grate the carrots, add to the sugar mix, and slowly fold in the flour, baking powder, and cinnamon.

5 Divide the mixture between the two pans.

6 Bake both cakes for 40 minutes.

7 Turn the cakes out onto a cooling rack and leave to cool. Then put in the fridge for 20 minutes.

8 For the icing, cube the butter, add the powdered sugar, and beat together using an electric mixer.

9 When smooth, add the vanilla extract and half the cream cheese and mix until smooth. Then add the rest of the cream cheese and mix in.

10 Whizz the graham crackers in a food processor until the mixture looks like sand.

11 Neatly cut the edges off both cakes to make 2 squares (save the edges for your turrets).

12 Sandwich the cakes with about one-third of the icing. Spread another third of the icing all over the top and sides.

13 Sprinkle the crushed graham cracker all over so it looks like a sandcastle.

14 Cut the leftover pieces of cake into turrets. Spread with the remaining icing, cover in graham cracker "sand," and fix to your sandcastle using toothpicks.

15 Use marzipan to make shell decorations. Cut little triangles out of rice paper, moisten with some water, and wrap them around the toothpicks to make flags.

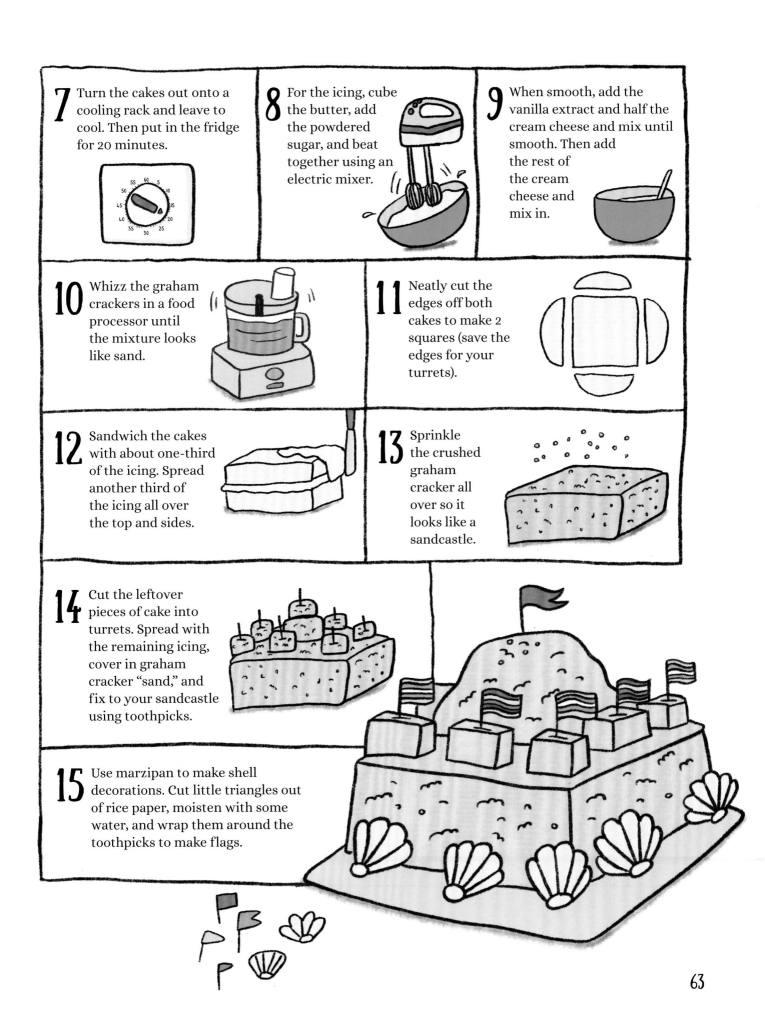

Ingredients

Cake

3 cups granulated sugar

3 ⅓ cups all-purpose flour

½ cup cocoa powder

4 tsp baking powder

¾ cup milk

⅔ cup vegetable oil

4 medium eggs

1 ⅓ cups water

2 tsp vanilla extract

1 tsp peppermint extract

Middle Icing

1 large sweet potato
  (about 8 oz)

⅓ cup cocoa powder

1 tsp vanilla extract

¾ cup powdered sugar

Top Icing

¾ cup granulated sugar

¾ cup cocoa powder

⅓ cup cornstarch

¾ cup water

2 tsp vanilla extract

1 ½ tbsp unsalted butter

Decorations

4 oz marzipan

6 raspberries

6 strawberries

Sprigs of fresh mint

Makes 14–16 servings

AUTUMN WOODLAND CAKE

I love going for walks in the forest and looking up at the trees. Now imagine if everything was made of chocolate! This recipe gives you the basic forest floor, but you can make other edible plants, insects, or leaves to create a woodland wonderland.

Method

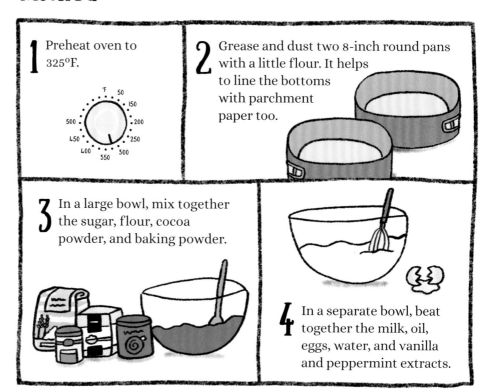

1 Preheat oven to 325°F.

2 Grease and dust two 8-inch round pans with a little flour. It helps to line the bottoms with parchment paper too.

3 In a large bowl, mix together the sugar, flour, cocoa powder, and baking powder.

4 In a separate bowl, beat together the milk, oil, eggs, water, and vanilla and peppermint extracts.

5 Pour the milk mixture into the flour mixture and beat until smooth.

6 Divide the mixture between the two pans and bake for 20–25 minutes (until a skewer comes out clean).

7 Allow the cakes to cool, then chill in the fridge for 20 minutes.

8 Peel, chop, and then boil the sweet potato for 10 minutes.

9 Put the cooked sweet potato into a measuring cup with the cocoa powder, vanilla extract, and powdered sugar. Blitz with an immersion blender until smooth.

10 Trim the top off the cakes so that they are flat (keep the cake cutoffs for later). Remove the parchment paper, and sandwich the cakes together with the potato icing.

11 Mix the sugar, cocoa powder, cornstarch, water, vanilla extract, and butter in a saucepan over a gentle heat. Keep stirring until smooth and slightly thickened.

12 Carefully pour the hot chocolate sauce over the cake and allow to set.

13 Make little stalks out of the marzipan, then stick a raspberry on top. Hollow out the strawberries and stick stalks into these too.

14 Crumble up the cake cutoffs and sprinkle on top of the cake as soil. Add the raspberry and strawberry "mushrooms," and stick in the sprigs of mint. Make little marzipan creatures too!

Ingredients

Cake

⅔ cup granulated sugar

5 tbsp unsalted butter (cubed, at room temperature)

3 large eggs

1 ¾ cups ground almonds

½ cup self-rising flour

1 tsp almond extract

1 small carrot

1 cup frozen raspberries

Icing

⅓ cup granulated sugar

⅓ cup cocoa powder

3 tbsp cornstarch

⅓ cup water

1 tsp vanilla extract

1 tbsp unsalted butter

Decoration

12 chocolate discs

Frozen raspberries

Silver balls (without gelatin)

12 mini pretzels

Makes 12 cakes

WINTER REINDEER PUDS

These sticky puddings are perfect if you're having a festive party. No one can resist a Santa's little helper cake!

Method

1 Preheat oven to 350°F.

2 Whisk the sugar and butter in a mixing bowl.

3 Add the eggs and keep whisking (it will look curdled, but don't worry).

4 Stir in the ground almonds, flour, and almond extract.

5 Finely grate the carrot and mix this through.

6 Grease a 12-hole muffin tin with butter and drop 3–4 frozen raspberries into each hole.

7 Spoon the mixture equally into the holes.

8 Bake for 15 minutes.

9 Allow to cool on a cooling rack upside down and make a start on your icing.

10 Mix the sugar, cocoa powder, cornstarch, water, vanilla extract, and butter in a saucepan over a gentle heat.

11 Keep stirring until smooth and slightly thickened (if it goes lumpy, take it off the heat and whizz it with an immersion blender).

12 Carefully remove the puddings from the tin. Pour the hot chocolate sauce over the cakes.

13 Cut the chocolate discs in half and place them at the top of your cakes for ears.

14 Add a defrosted raspberry for the nose and silver balls for the eyes.

15 Just before serving, snap a pretzel in half and stick into your cake to make antlers!

ABOUT DAVID AND ALICE

David Atherton is the 2019 winner of *The Great British Baking Show*. David's first cookbook for children, *Bake, Make, and Learn to Cook*, inspired young cooks to create healthy, imaginative recipes for their friends and family. David is a food writer and an international health adviser for a charity. He has worked on health programs around the world and never misses an opportunity to explore a new food culture. David is passionate about ensuring that children grow up as food lovers and understand how to make tasty, healthy food.

Alice Bowsher is a London-based illustrator who works primarily with chunky black ink to create joyful characters, large-scale murals, and illustrated sets. The imagery she produces is simple, playful, and intriguing, full of quick spontaneous marks.